She Believes

75
Devotionals to Encourage, Motivate, and Inspire

Krystle Ashley Barrington

Unless otherwise identified, Scripture quotations are from the New International Version of the Bible. Scriptures taken from the HOLY BIBLE, NEW INTERNATIONAL VERSION®. Copyright © 1937, 1978, 1984 by International Bible Society. Used by permission of Zondervan Publishing House. All rights reserved. Scripture quotations noted from the ESV® Bible (The Holy Bible, English Standard Version®), copyright © 2001 by Crossway, a publishing ministry of Good News Publishers. Used by permission. All rights reserved. Scripture quotations from NIV, Holy Bible, New Living Translation, copyright (c) 1996, 2004, 2007 by Tyndale House Foundation. Used by permission of Tyndale House Publishers, Inc., Carol Stream, Illinois 60188. All rights reserved. Scripture quotations noted KJV are from the King James Version.

Edited by Val Pugh
Cover Design by Ana Grigoriu
Interior Design by Leslie Allen

Printed in the United States of America
First Printing, 2015
ISBN 978-0-9967085-0-0 (paperback)
ISBN 978-0-9967085-1-7 (e-book)
Chasing Butterflies Publishing

If you would like to use material from the book (other than for review purposes), please direct your inquiries to: chasingbutterfliespublishing@gmail.com.

Printed in the United States

Acknowledgements

To my friends and family: I love and appreciate you.

To my parents: Thank you for calling me an author before I wrote one word of this book. Thank you for praying for me and always encouraging me.

A special shout out to **my father** who spent many hours explaining scripture to me and pouring into me. I will always cherish those moments.

To my mom and sister: Thank you for always believing in my abilities. You two will always be my favorite girls.

To Cara, Karla, Camille, Deidre, Alaina, Stephanie, Jennifer, Ijeoma, and Ucheena: Thank you for being true friends during this process.

To anyone that I've missed: Please charge it to my mind and not my heart.

Contents

Introduction

This book is a dream come true. The process of writing it has been a huge blessing to me in so many ways, but getting here wasn't easy. The topics discussed are largely inspired by my own struggles in life - some of which I am still facing. This book is my testimony. The fact that you are reading something that I wrote is my testimony. The fact that I started this project and finished it while having struggled with self-doubt throughout my entire life is my testimony. The majority of this book was written a few years ago, but I was too afraid to share it. In addition to having no knowledge on self-publishing, it felt like such a daunting task, so I let it sit. Life went on, and God gave me specific instructions to get off my behind and stop being afraid. When you've talked about doing something for so long and you never do it, it's easy to just let your dream die. After a while, it becomes easy to act like you never uttered a word about what God called you to be. The thing is, God won't forget.

I don't remember a time I didn't know of God. I grew up in church and I learned to love God as a child, but I don't think I truly felt God's presence until I was fifteen years old. It was the day after I had major spinal surgery. I remember like yesterday waking up the next morning and feeling God so much that tears fell down my face. I knew that He protected me during that five-hour surgery. I knew it was He who had control over those doctors' hands. He protected me. He covered me on that operating table, and I was grateful. The joy I felt that day will never be matched. I recovered and went on to high school - a very awkward time in my life. I was extremely shy, and I'd developed a complex that I wasn't good enough - something that would haunt me for many years.

When I went off to college, I attended church on a regular basis, but my life's choices were a sad cry from righteous. I had more than enough fun to go around. In some ways, I found myself, yet in so many other ways, I was dangerously lost. I had one foot in and one foot out, straddled the proverbial fence, if you will. God was a small part of my life, and while I called Him "my every-thing," He was low on my priority list. Through all of my deci-sions, both righteous and unrighteous, God stuck with me. I graduated from college, and I'm in the real world now. Work life brought its own set of challenges, of course, and I found myself needing God in ways I never needed Him before. My attitude, my patience, and the ability to not let my environment change me be-came a real life daily struggle.

Things got better over the years, but we all know that sea-sons change and sometimes come right back around. Life was going well at work. I received one promotion after another. I felt like my career was headed in a good direction, but the tests just kept on coming, and they're still coming today. Opportunities I prayed for came with more headaches than I could have imagined. I guess new opportunities plus challenges are a package deal. However, experience has taught me that while we would love for life to be perfect, there is no way God can reveal Himself to us if we never face any trials. While trying to figure out my career, my heart faced many battles as well. I settled and let my emotions, rather than the Spirit of God, drive my decisions. I decided I was tired of setting myself up for disappointment, so I took a long look in the mirror and had to accept some hard truths about myself. From there, my life started to change.

My relationship with God changed when I stopped forcing friendships and relationships. I stopped chasing after love and started to find rest in God's presence. I removed clutter from my life, and I could see things so much more clearly. I started to give my time back to God so much that without quiet time to meditate on His word, I just didn't feel right.

I'm on the best ride of my life, and I'm fighting tooth and nail to stay on track. I will never reach perfection, but I want to be filled by God's presence day in and day out. It's a process, and I am far from where I need to be. However, by God's grace, I have come a long way. I like to think that the closer we get to God, the more equipped we are in making decisions in our daily lives. We have the responsibility to make God priority. The world we live in doesn't care that we love God. The distractions will never stop. Our flesh wants what it wants. What's stopping you from doing what you've been called to do? Don't experience blessings five years from now that you should have had ten years ago, simply because you are afraid of the process. Moments of feeling fear is natural, but to live in fear is paralyzing. The process might be tough, and there will be mistakes and setbacks, but you, my dear, are a conqueror.

As we mature as women, life will get busier, and responsibilities will continue to increase. However, no matter how hectic life gets, we still have to make time for God. For the woman who doesn't believe that her situation can get better, know that who we are and where we come from is not a liability but an opportunity to rise above. Many times, we are faced with circumstances far beyond our comprehension. As a result, we question our purpose, our dreams, and our abilities. What if I told you that underneath all the pain, frustration, confusion, and struggles that life creates, you are still equipped to be great? Well, it's true!

The road to being a confident Christian woman is unique for all of us. It is a never-ending journey with peaks and valleys along the way. Wherever you are in your walk with God, it is my hope that you learn something about yourself and God as you read through this book. It is meant to be the beginning of the rest of your journey with God. By learning to see yourself through God's eyes, I pray that you will develop new confidence and new determinations to keep pushing through life. The more we discover about God, the more prepared we are for life.

No matter how far we might stray from God, He is never far from us, because He promised He'd never leave nor forsake us. God will never turn us away when we run back into His arms. It's my mission to remind you that even in all of our mess, God will always be in our corner. It is my prayer and hope that as you read this book, you will be encouraged, enlightened, and inspired to be the best woman of God you can be.

With Love,

Krystle A. Barrington

1- A Renewed Mind

"Do not conform to the pattern of this world, but be transformed by renewing your mind. Then, you will be able to test and approve what God's will is – His good and perfect will." (Romans 12:2)

Our mindset has the power to push us forward or hold us back. We can literally waste our thoughts on things and people who are not good for us. We can talk ourselves out of pursuing our dreams or doing things we've always wanted to do. We can even tell ourselves that we aren't special and that we don't deserve the things God has for us. Our thoughts have extreme power over our attitudes, our behaviors, and our approaches toward situations. I once had a job that I wasn't happy with, and I honestly thought I was going to lose my mind. I convinced myself that I had made a horrible mistake by taking the job, and my attitude and willingness to even try diminished more and more each day. Rather than give up and accept defeat, I needed to speak over the job, the training, and my ability to do the job. My mindset at the time held me back.

"Death and life are in the power of the tongue, and those who love it will eat its fruits." (Proverbs 18:21 ESV)

Whether you realize it or not, you have the ability to redirect your thoughts. You can decide today to be mindful of how you approach situations in life. Yes, life gets hard, and sometimes nothing seems to be going right, but you can choose to speak life into your situation. You can choose to hold onto God's promises and approach life with a new determination. When we feel like a pity party is coming on, we have to remind ourselves that we can indeed overcome anything we face when we trust in God. Don't be afraid to be positive because you don't want to feel disappointment. Instead, keep on claiming victory and trusting in God. No harm will ever come from doing so.

2-Self Doubt

"I can do all things through Christ who strengthens me."
(Philippians 4:13 NKJ)

How we view ourselves influences many things, including our role in relationships, our confidence, and our ability to see things through. While it may be difficult at times, we have to define ourselves the way God sees us. Our mission is to please God in everything that we do, and that includes how we view ourselves. For me, being teased at a very young age really made me grow up with this complex that I wasn't enough. That mindset followed me for so many years and influenced my life in great ways that led to dysfunctional relationships and running away from great opportunities. I finally had to say to myself, "You can spend your entire life doubting your ability to do great things, or you can trust that with God, you can do anything." Where we are lacking, God surely fills those gaps. If the bible tells us that we can do all things through Christ, we should walk with our heads held high. You are who He says you are. Don't fight it. Don't deny it. Accept it and live by it each and every day.

3- Real Change

"Trust in the Lord with all your heart and lean not on your own understanding; in all your ways acknowledge Him, and He will make your paths straight." (Proverbs 3:5-6)

Have you ever tried to make a huge change in your life and found yourself doing really well for a while, but then you fell right back into that old habit? Have you considered that it could be because you embarked on trying to make this change, but you didn't take God along with you? I know I am guilty of this, and life lessons have taught me that real change comes from discipline and seeking God daily. Trying to make a permanent change without God is essentially leaning on our own understanding.

As you continue to read, a common theme will be intentionality and the idea that we cannot be passive about seeking God, especially when we are trying to make significant changes that will strengthen our relationship with Him. The devil is always, yes always, looking for an opportunity to test us. Sometimes, it's not until we really decide to make a positive change that we start to catch some real hell. When we go through life with God, we have a fighting chance to do better. You don't have to do it alone. I encourage you to lean on Him and His word, and watch how much easier the fight will be.

4- Go Getter

"In the same way, faith by itself, if it is not accompanied by action, is dead." (James 2:17)

We all aspire to be something, and no matter what that something is, we cannot get there without faith, determination, and some good old hard work. No one can deny that women of today are leaders, business owners, and doing pretty much anything that men can do. This is evidence that we can be anything we want to be. The thing is, we can talk about doing something all we want. We can even pray until we are blue in the face, that all of our dreams and hopes will come to pass. The truth is, unless we put in some work, none of the above will happen. Yes, God is still in the business of working out miracles, but a business plan will not write itself. A vision will not come to reality just by talking about it. We have to put some action behind our dreams and hopes.

Get out the house and connect with other like-minded people. Become knowledgeable about the industry you may be interested in, by taking classes and attending networking events. Do what you have to do in order to be successful. You should definitely write down your goals and pray on them every chance you get. However, don't forget to do the work, and don't expect anything to be handed to you. If it means getting out of your comfort zone, so be it. If God gave you a vision, He will surely be there with you every step of the way, but you've got to get to work.

5- Keep Doing Good Works

"Let us not become weary in doing good, for at the proper time we will reap a harvest if we do not give up. Therefore, as we have opportunity, let us do good to all people, especially to those who belong to the family of believers." (Galatians 6:9-10)

Does it sometimes seem like doing the right thing isn't getting you anywhere? You sit back and watch others do the bare minimum only for them to experience continued success. It seems like you take ten steps forward towards bettering yourself only to see someone else cutting corners and getting to the finish line first. Or, maybe you're going out of your way to help others and never really seem to get a thank you.

Well, remember that we should never focus on what we can see with our own eyes. Keep doing right by people. Not only does the scripture tell us that our actions are not going unnoticed, but it also says that we will reap a harvest in due time. Keep doing things the honest way. Keep chasing after the right things. If it seems like no one else sees your good deeds, let me assure you that God hears all and sees all.

6- That Thing Called Faith

"Therefore we do not lose heart. Though outwardly we are wasting away, yet inwardly we are being renewed day by day. For our light and momentary troubles are achieving for us an eternal glory that far outweighs them all. So we fix our eyes not on what is seen, but on what is unseen, since what is seen is temporary, but what is unseen is eternal." (2 Corinthians 4:16-18)

One of the scriptures that I absolutely love is Hebrews 11:1. It reads, "Faith is the substance of things hoped for, the evidence of things unseen." These are such powerful words that are the essence of our walk with God. Sometimes, it is unbelievably difficult to see how a situation is going to get better because it seems to continue to get worse. I mean, who really wants to be tested from every angle? Who wants to trust that when backed against the wall, things are going to get better? Does He really want us to believe that everything will work out for the good when everything is falling apart? Yes, yes, yes, that is correct, and sometimes I don't like how it feels myself. Life gets tough and sometimes hoping and praying for relief is a test in itself, but God's word tells us to do just that. Many times, we stare at what we really ought to just glance at. We glance at God, but stare at our problems. Instead, we should focus on God, so that He can change our perspective on things.

What is seen: No available jobs. No growth in the workplace. Business isn't growing fast enough. Relationship is going through tough times. Friendships are broken. Financial situation is the worst it's ever been. I could go on and on and on when it comes to the troubles that we have experienced, that we are experiencing right now, and that are waiting for us next week. My point is simply that, we cannot serve God without faith. As Christians, we have to get to a place where we view circumstances as opportunities to pray, to grow, and to see God work. We have to take the focus off of our problems and have faith in God. In order for faith to grow, it needs resistance. The good news is that there is always victory on the other side of our problems. What we have to do is declare victory no matter what we are facing. We must seek God's word daily, so that we are continually reminded that things will work out for the best.

7- From Blessing to Burden to Blessing

"And we know that in all things God works for the good of those who love Him, who have been called according to His purpose." *(Romans 8:28)*

Isn't it a blessing when we ask God for something and we get it? We call everybody we can to tell them the good news. Then, after a while, the excitement dies down a bit, and things don't seem so perfect anymore. Let me give you an example. I had gotten a promotion, and I was so excited. It was the next step in my career in my mind and in reality. Well, training was a complete disaster. In addition, in order for me to meet the job requirements, I would work ten hours a day Monday through Friday, and if I could have taken work home, I probably would have. I went from jumping for joy to crying in my car on my lunch break. I asked God, "Why would you give me this job if you knew what I'd have to deal with?" His answer was clear after months of the same thing, "Because you can't live life without me, Krystle."

I had prayed for that job and believed that it was mine, only to get it and experience what I considered to be hell on earth at the time. I got so pissed off at God that I stopped going to church. I stopped tithing. I didn't want to hear anything about God. As months went by, my anger turned into sadness, and even though I fought it, I had to tell God there was no way I could learn the job without Him. I asked God to forgive me for my attitude, because I knew that having a bad attitude is like a flat tire, and I wasn't going anywhere until I fixed it. Day by day, I found myself giving all my stress and worry back to God.

Things did not get better overnight, but once I realized that God would never set me up for failure, my perspective on the situation changed. My situation told me that I'd failed, and when things didn't get any better, my faith diminished. Yet, the experience served as an opportunity to trust in God and to exercise my faith. God has never and will never put His children in a situation that we will not learn and grow from. There is a purpose in every situation we face, and we just have to be willing to go through the process with some faith. We must be willing to see situations from God's perspective.

8- Who Do You Choose?

"He who walks with the wise grows wise, but a companion of fools suffers harm." (Proverbs 13:20)

When we decide we want to know God on a deeper level, we have to realize that not everyone, not every habit, and not every desire can go with us. As such, one of the hardest things to do a Christian is to let go of things that we want and enjoy in our lives, even when they don't add value to our walk with God. The bible is so accurate when it says we cannot serve two masters. If we say that God is first in our lives or that He is the most important, our actions should reflect this. Instead, everyone and everything else seems to take first place.

To intentionally seek God is to intentionally walk away from those things and people that have a strong hold on us. We cannot chase the things of this world yet claim that God is most important, because that just isn't possible. When we sincerely give our minds, our bodies, our gifts, our talents, our careers, and our hearts to God, it will blow our minds away. I am convinced that I've only seen a mere glimpse of who God is, and I just want to know and experience Him so much more. He is the strength we have when we are weak and low. He is our peace of mind when hell is all around us. He is our protector. He is our friend. He is whatever we need whenever we need it.

We might say, to walk away sounds good, but how exactly do we do it? Personally, I'd suggest that we run rather than walk. The quicker we get away from our hindrances, the closer we will be to reaching a deeper level with God. First, we have to identify what we ought to be running from as we work towards growing with God. Once we determine what that is or who that is, then we can really start to become disciplined and intentional in our day to day decisions. After that, we have to relinquish leading our own lives, because that's what got us in trouble in the first place. God is always available and accessible, and we have to depend on His supernatural help. So, if the Holy Spirit is leading us in a new direction, we have to follow, because that is His way of helping us run away from our invaluable distractions.

9- A Deeper Relationship

"That the God of our Lord Jesus Christ, the Father of glory, may give to you a Spirit of wisdom and of revelation in the knowledge of Him." (Ephesians 1:17 KJV)

It is very possible to live an entire lifetime and never know God on a deeper level. Surface level religion is often appealing and comes at no cost to us. It allows us to live as we please and give our time and efforts to things that we desire, rather than to God. That level of religion was my reality for many years. Through my experiences on that level, I learned that we have to make sacrifices to really learn more about God. Furthermore, we have to grow wiser in who God is and how we should live as we walk with God.

For as long as I can remember, my father has always encouraged me to seek God, to pray, to read the word, and to spend intimate and uninterrupted time with God. He always told me that the benefits of truly seeking God are endless. He is right! Just as Paul encouraged the church of Ephesus to know God better, my father has encouraged me to seek God more, as well. So, I want to encourage you to get to know Him better. The wisdom and revelation that comes from developing a deeper relationship with God is absolutely priceless. There is always something new to learn and discover about God. Even if it's reading a bible story or thinking over a scripture you may have heard countless times, give God the opportunity to speak into your life in new ways. You won't regret it.

10- Comparing Success

"Each one should test their own actions. Then they can take pride in themselves alone, without comparing themselves to someone else." (Galatians 6:4)

How successful we are should not be compared to the success of others. As we mature, it is extremely important for us to be grateful and content with every single blessing we receive from God. Moreover, we should never dismiss our achievements because they don't measure up to what society defines as successful. You are successful in your own right, and you should own all of your accomplishments, no matter how small others may perceive them to be. Success in the economy of God and success in the economy of man are different feats. Even if you can't afford the latest and the greatest, be grateful for what you do have.

If we fixate on what others have and how others are living, we may begin to question our own success. Remember, the blessings that God has for you are specifically for you. They were designed specifically for your talents, your unique creativity, and your individuality. Own your success and be proud. Thank God for where you are and for your current accomplishments. Keep putting in work to do better, but don't forget to thank Him for your success to date.

11- Stamp of Approval

"I can do everything through Him who gives me strength."
(Philippians 4:13)

God's vision for your life doesn't require approval by others. Not everyone is going to understand why you want to pursue a particular goal. Frankly, not everyone is going to support you. There is nothing like someone close to you dismissing your goals. Their lack of support can be quite discouraging, but the reality is that they don't need to see your vision in order for it to come to pass. One opinion doesn't change your potential or your destiny. Remember, when God gives you a vision, it doesn't require someone else's approval.

There are always going to be people who try to talk you out of pursuing your goals. The thing is, they want you to do well, just not better than they're doing. They want you to be successful, but they don't want to see you successful before they are. Keep in mind that when you share your dreams with people and they aren't encouraging, there is a good chance that they aren't praying for you and your vision. Guess what? That's okay, because when God gives you a vision, you don't need their encouragement, because you've already gotten His approval. There isn't a devil in hell that could ever keep you from seeing your dreams come to pass when God is involved. So, don't let whispers keep you from being bold in your pursuits. Don't allow unsupportive people to make you shy away from doing what God has told you to do. The more people try to hold you back, the more you ought to pray. The more people try to discourage you, the more you ought to speak your goals into existence. Even if you can't see it with your eyes, believe it in your heart. Don't allow people to make you doubt your God-given vision. Own your dreams. Own your aspirations. Own the process.

12- Fruit for the Moody

"But the fruit of the Spirit is love, joy, peace, patience, kindness, goodness, faithfulness, gentleness, and self-control. Against such things there is no law." (Galatians 5:22-23)

I can't be the only person who sometimes finds herself in a sour mood for no reason at all. Sometimes, I literally just want to be left alone, and I don't want to be bothered. I don't want anyone calling me. I don't want anyone asking me silly questions. I just want to be in my own little world. Sounds a little like being moody to me, right? Better yet, have you ever felt a million and one emotions all in one day? You woke up happy, but when you got to work you were instantly irritated. Then, maybe your beau called and you were giggly, but by the time you hung up the phone, you had an attitude again.

The scripture tells us that even on our worst day, we should be led by the Spirit and not our flesh. Our flesh might want to tell everyone to approach with caution, but we are commanded to be led by the Spirit. To be led by the Spirit is to show love, joy, peace, patience, kindness, goodness, and faithfulness. These are all things that are worth practicing. When we feel ourselves starting to feel some kind of way, we should stop in our tracks and ask God to help us readjust our attitude at that moment. When we do this, we can instantly begin to have a softer heart. We might have to pray every five minutes, but it is certainly possible for us to get through the day in better spirits.

13- Bruises Don't Fade Overnight

"If we confess our sins, He is faithful and just and will forgive us our sins and purify us from all unrighteousness." (1 John 1:9)

We've all done things we aren't proud that we did. Unfortunately, we can't erase our past decisions. We can't erase the opportunities that we didn't go after, nor can we erase the time we spent chasing after people and things that were not good for us. Because of poor decisions, I spent so much time hiding in the background over the years that I found myself running from my purpose. For a long time, I walked around beating myself up because I couldn't get back the time I spent wallowing in self-pity. Instead of running after things that brought me temporary happiness, I could have been writing this book! Before I could heal from my past, I had to accept God's forgiveness. More importantly, I had to sit down and examine the decisions that I made so that I could make better choices in the future.

Whatever happened in your past that is hindering you from moving forward, I encourage you to let it go. It's especially difficult when the decisions we make affect other people. Thank God that our mistakes don't define us! Past hurts, failed relationships, wasting precious time on trivial things, settling in life, and many other disappointments can be the very entity that will lead you to victory. Every single mistake we make in life can be a lesson learned and an opportunity to walk away from a situation and towards God. The bruises of our past may not fade overnight, but when we accept God's forgiveness, it can bring peace that allows us to heal.

Mistakes are roadblocks, but they don't define who we are or how great we will be. Don't allow shame and guilt to hold you hostage. God's forgiveness is real, and we have to accept His forgiveness, forgive ourselves, and continue towards our destiny. Start your journey to rebuilding your life by praying this prayer at this very moment: "Lord, I did some things that I am not proud of, and I feel so ashamed. Your word says that nothing can separate me from your love, so I ask that you forgive me for my sins. Thank you for love, forgiveness, and mercy. Amen."

14- Who is Your Teacher?

"For the time is coming when people will not endure sound teaching, but having itching ears they will accumulate for themselves teachers to suit their own passions, and will turn away from listening to the truth and wander off into myths." (2 Timothy 4:3-4 ESV)

Throughout my journey of life, I've drifted far away from God along the way. At times, I was so caught up in what I wanted at the time that I didn't want to hear anything about what God's word said I should be doing. If I spent time with God, that meant He'd convict me in my heart for my actions. Therefore, I drew closer to things and people that only encouraged me to chase after my own selfish desires. Sadly, when we are set on doing our own thing, we have a tendency of shifting priorities and finding every excuse to do as we please. Oh, what a scary place to be!

We have to be mindful of who and what we allow to influence our lives. Who is feeding your soul? Who is directing your decisions? Who is influencing the person you want to be? Make no mistake, if God is not influencing you, the devil is, no matter how sweet, pretty, or handsome it may be. As I have gotten older and a bit wiser, I have learned the true value of having people close to me who understand the necessity to grow closer to God. I appreciate those "teachers" I have in my life who remind me, especially when I am drifting away from God, that close to Him is where I need to be.

15- The Good, the Bad, & the Ugly

"Yet, oh Lord, you are our Father. We are the clay, you are the potter; we are all the work of your hand." (Isaiah 64:8)

Self-discovery is so important in maturing as a woman. In order for God to mold us, we have to be honest about our issues and seek God's guidance. While constructive feedback from someone we're close to is a positive thing, and sometimes very necessary, I think it is always appropriate to have quiet time with God to reflect, to evaluate, and to identify issues we might be running from in our lives. Life gets busy, and responsibilities seem to be a mile long. Before we know it, quiet time with God has been pushed to the side while we take care of ourselves and our responsibilities. In actuality, time with God is your way of taking care of yourself. If you neglect yourself, you surely can't take care of anyone else to the best of your ability. To others, you may appear to have your life in order, and you may have made yourself believe the same. The truth is, sometimes we just need time to focus on the good, the bad, and the ugly in order to grow as a person. We all have things we need to work on, but if we don't acknowledge those things, we will never overcome them.

So, what is your truth? What is inauthentic about your life? What do you need to change in order to treat yourself better? How can you better serve God? These are all questions we have to ask ourselves not once, not twice, but on a regular basis. Lying to ourselves daily is just as tragic as someone else lying to our faces day in and day out. Examine your life and take notes of the areas that need improvement. Embrace the good, but acknowledge and work on the bad and especially the ugly. It might be hard to face your truth, but it will be so worth it in the end.

16- What Are You Focusing On?

"Finally brothers, whatever is true, whatever is honorable, whatever is just, whatever is pure, whatever is lovely, whatever is commendable, if there is any excellence, if there is anything worthy of praise, think about these things." (Philippians 4:8 ESV)

This scripture tells us that we should focus on things that are true, honorable, pure, lovely, commendable, excellent, and worthy of praise. This means that our focus should be on those things that are good and positive in our lives. It doesn't mean to ignore our issues or problems but we cannot let them consume us. We should make an effort to replace our negative thoughts with positive thoughts. I know firsthand that negative thinking comes from a place of doubt and fear, and many times the worse things look, the worse our attitude can get. Remember, we have to take our focus off of what we can see with our eyes and focus on where faith can take us. If we focus on the negative, it is like planting a bad seed and then watering it regularly while expecting good harvest from it. We are setting ourselves up for disappointment, because we still expect a positive outcome yet we have energized the negativity. Do not be afraid to exercise faith in all situations. Faith is a positive attribute that is pleasing to God. To the negative eye, if we are missing something in life, we should not be happy with the few things that we do have. However, God's word tells us that if we are faithful over few, He will make us ruler over many. So, be positive, have faith, and try not to focus on the negative. This will please God, and you will be rewarded for your effort.

17- God's Wisdom

"For the foolishness of God is wiser than man's wisdom, and the weakness of God is stronger than man's strength."
(1 Corinthians 1:25)

Sometimes the best advice or the most logical solution to a problem is not always what God's word tells us to do. The more we read our bibles, the more we will see through scripture that God's wisdom cannot be matched. What He commands of us is spiritual and not logical. Forgive those who hurt us? Be kind to those who have been ugly to us? Show grace and mercy to some-one who has wronged us? Do you see where I am going with this? As Christians, we need to be mindful of who we seek advice from and remember that every bit of advice we are given may not be worth entertaining. In the same way that we don't want others to feed us nonsense or stroke our egos, we also have to be mindful of the type of advice we give to others. Are we giving advice that falls in line with God's word, or are we giving advice that sounds good? The advice we give should be led by the Spirit and not by what feels right at the time or by what simply sounds good. Let us re-member that God is spiritual and not logical.

18- What is New Becomes Old

"Do not lay up for yourselves treasures on earth, where moth and rust destroy and where thieves break in and steal, but lay up for yourselves treasures in heaven, where neither moth nor rust destroys and where thieves do not break in and steal. For where your treasure is, there your heart will be also." (Matthew 6:19-21)

Have you ever bought something, loved it, and then over time, you forgot it existed? Then, one day when you are in a mood for organizing, you stumble upon what "used" to be your favorite pair of shoes, purse, dress, etc. I'm so guilty of this that it's ridiculous! It's so funny how we can value something for a little while, and then forget it even exists. The thing is, everything that is new eventually becomes old. It loses its value literally, or maybe it just doesn't fit our needs anymore. So, we throw it to the side, or it gets buried under more stuff that we will eventually forget about as well.

The reality is that we ought to never worship or idolize anything that we own. Instead, we must worship God and spend time with Him just as we do with our new favorite items. Unlike those material things, God will never become old and valueless, and He will always bring newness to our lives. Our hearts should never be torn between God and something that hasn't saved us. What do you treasure and why? What is in your heart? Having nice things is certainly okay, but we must always remember that "things" are just "things" and everything we have is really on loan from God.

19- The Holy Spirit

"Do you not know that you are a temple of God and that the Spirit of God dwells in you?" (1 Corinthians 3:16 ESV)

The Father, the Son, and the Holy Spirit are at the core of Christianity. God, our Father, gave His only darling Son, Jesus Christ, to die on the cross for our sins, but He didn't leave us alone. He sent the Holy Spirit here to be with us on earth, so that we would always be connected to the Father and to the Son of God. As Christians, I think we sometimes forget that God literally lives inside of us. That's right, the Spirit of God lives inside each of us!

Did you know that when something troubles you so much that you can't eat or sleep, it is in those moments that God wants you to know that you have something in you that can and will help you along the way? Simply, God is always with us, because He lives in us. When we learn that the God who loves us actually lives within us and wants the best for us, we should develop a confidence and an assurance that everything will be okay. He will give us what we need and enable us to see things from His perspective, and in that, we have the victory!

20- The Art of Giving

"Remember this: Whoever sows sparingly will also reap sparingly, and whoever sows generously will also reap generously. Each man should give what he has decided in his heart to give, not reluctantly or under compulsion, for God loves a cheerful giver."
(2 Corinthians 9:6-7)

The more we are blessed by God, the more we should be a blessing to others. Our giving should not be predicated on what we can get from God, but based on the fact that God has already been very good to us. The scripture takes it a step further and says that if you cannot give with a good heart or you have to be persuaded, you shouldn't give. People often believe that giving is limited to money, but we can give to people in so many other ways. It could simply be mentoring someone, volunteering, or even sharing information with others. Giving should never have stipulations or be done grudgingly. No matter how we choose to bless others, we should always do it with a heart of love - God's love.

21- The Art of Listening

"My son, if you accept my words and store up my commands within you, turning your ear to wisdom and applying your heart to understanding, and if you call out for insight and cry aloud for understanding, and if you look for it as for silver and search for it as for hidden treasure, then you will understand the fear of the Lord and find the knowledge of God." (Proverbs 2:1-5)

Great communication is important in any relationship, and it is especially important in our relationship with God. One of the biggest challenges with communication is the lack of listening and the surplus of talking. Many times when someone is speaking to us, we have a response ready before they've finished expressing their thoughts, and it may even be accompanied with an attitude. Poor communication methods can also make it difficult for us to receive messages from God because it is often one-sided. We run to God with our problems, but we aren't always open to hearing what He has to say nor do we simply seek God to get closer to Him.

So, how do we learn to recognize when God is speaking to us? It starts with removing distractions from our lives and making a real effort to spend quiet time with God and His word. We cannot learn the wisdom of God, if we don't read it. We cannot apply it, if we don't hear it. We have to train ourselves to decipher His voice from all the noise going on around us. In addition, we have to train ourselves to talk to God not just when things are bad, but also when things are good. We don't like those friends who only call on us when they need something, right? Well, we need to keep that in mind when we call upon God. We have to discipline ourselves to communicate with God. In doing so, we will learn how to recognize His voice, and we will surely become wiser.

22- I See You

"Beware of practicing your righteousness before other people in order to be seen by them, for then you will have no reward from your Father who is in heaven." (Matthew 6:1 ESV)

This scripture commands us to do right, not for attention or a pat on our backs, but simply because that's what we are required to do. God knows when we are not authentic. He knows when our praise, our giving, our willingness to help others, etc. is not sincere. We can fool everyone else around us, but we cannot fool God. He desires for us to do things from a place of sincerity and obedience. When we do things out of a genuine desire to please God, the bible says that He will reward us in Heaven. Let us be authentic and sincere in doing what is right. God will see our sincerity, and He will reward us accordingly.

23- First Responder

"But seek first the kingdom of God and His righteousness, and all these things will be added to you." (Matthew 6:33 ESV)

At a very young age, we learn to pick up the phone and call our best friend when we need help. From there, we might make a few additional calls, before we even think to just pray. There is nothing wrong with getting someone's opinion; however, God wants us to seek Him first. We must learn to intentionally seek God so that He doesn't become an afterthought. Instead of seeking advice from everyone else, our first thought should be to pray. The good news is that when we choose to pray first, we don't have to wait for God to call us back or for Him to find time to respond to a text. He is readily available 24 hours a day and 365 days a year. He wants to be our first responder. Remember that God is a prayer away no matter the time or the place, and He's never too busy to hear from you.

24- Patiently Waiting

"Rest in the Lord, and wait patiently for Him." (Psalms 37:7 ESV)

God knows what we need and when we need it. Sometimes it's very convenient for us to settle for things in our lives because we don't exercise enough patience to wait on what God has for us. We make decisions without Him giving us consent to move forward. We lean on our own understanding, and do what feels right to us. Little do we realize, this often postpones our blessings. Just imagine how far we can go, if we learn to wait for God to tell us what our next move should be. Yes, waiting can get tiring, but there is a purpose in that season of our lives when we wait on God. This is when we have the opportunity to develop our trust in Him. Don't settle for what is convenient at the time, but wait with expectancy. Remember, patience is never developed, if we aren't put in a position to wait. Let your next move be your best move, because you were led by God.

25- Worry Not

"Do not be anxious about anything, but in every situation, by prayer and petition, with thanksgiving, present your requests to God." (Philippians 4:6)

If I could tell my younger self one thing, it would be to live in the moment. I've always struggled with worrying. I tend to internalize issues, instead of releasing them to God. It's something I continue to work on but it's no easy thing for me. We can choose to go through life worrying about tomorrow, or we can decide to live a life of joy today and every day. This happens when we focus on the good things and pray about those things we don't have control over. Philippians 4:6 tells us that in every situation, we ought to not only pray, but remain thankful. Worrying is focusing on that part of the glass that is half empty, and not being thankful for the part that is half full. Moreover, it can suck the life out of us and have us feeling down. I encourage you to give all your worries to God through prayer. I'm trying to do the same. He wants us to trust Him, and find peace in knowing that our prayers do not fall on deaf ears.

26 - Don't Forget

"The LORD Himself goes before you and will be with you; He will never leave you nor forsake you. Do not be afraid; do not be discouraged." (Deuteronomy 31:8)

When we are going through trials, one of the best ways to keep pushing through is to remember what God has already done for us. I'm a huge fan of journaling. Sometimes I will pick up a journal from a year or two ago, and I am quickly reminded that while I may not be where I want to be, I am far from where I used to be. God is the only constant force in our lives. Don't let your troubles overshadow all that God has done and continues to do for you. There is power in knowing that God will never leave us. The same God who protected you in the past is He who will protect you now. Be encouraged, because God is already working things out for you. He will not fail you.

27- Ready for Battle

"Finally, be strong in the Lord and in His mighty power. Put on the full armor of God, so that you can take your stand against the devil's schemes. For our struggle is not against flesh and blood, but against the rulers, against the authorities, against the powers of this dark world and against the spiritual forces of evil in the heavenly realms. Therefore, put on the full armor of God, so that when the day of evil comes, you may be able to stand your ground, and after you have done everything, to stand. Stand firm then, with the belt of truth buckled around your waist, with the breastplate of righteousness in place, and with your feet fitted with the readiness that comes from the gospel of peace. In addition to all this, take up the shield of faith, with which you can extinguish all the flaming arrows of the evil one. Take the helmet of salvation and the sword of the Spirit, which is the word of God." (Ephesians 6:10-17)

I can think of no greater place than the workplace to put on the full armor of God. Some of the most trying times in my life have been associated with working and trying to find my way professionally. You may have encountered some of the same situations I've faced on my journey. Leadership might be poor. Your hard work is never appreciated. The environment is draining. The workplace is just one example, but every single day we are faced with evil, and if we aren't ready, we will surely lose the battle.

My question to you is: are you ready for battle? Are you relying on the Holy Spirit to get you through life? Are you wearing the full armor of God? Or, are you shield ready without your helmet? Are you breast plate ready without readied feet? A soldier is never ready for battle without his full armor. Every day is a battle on the battlefield of life. To be victorious, we must constantly wear the full armor of God which includes meditating on His word and relying on it in every situation.

28- Blind Faith

"Now faith is being sure of what we hope for and certain of what we do not see." (Hebrews 11:1)

Any woman with a God-given vision has to have blind faith. You can't see it. You can't even fully imagine it. Yet, He has called you to believe in whatever that "it" may be for you. An example of blind faith is when you have dreams, but you may not have the contacts or the funds to achieve your goals, yet God still says to believe. Believe that He can make a way. Believe that He can connect you with the right people. Believe that He will equip you with everything you need to be successful. Believe that it will come to pass. You might get a few doors slammed in your face, but the next door just might be your big break. So, keep the faith, and don't give up. Some doors that are slammed in your face may be a *good thing* that sets you up for *God's best thing*.

29- Perfectly Imperfect

*"He is the Rock, His works are perfect, and all His ways are just. A faithful God who does no wrong, upright and just He is."
(Deuteronomy 32:4)*

A genuine love for God and a sincere desire to live according to His word cannot and will not make us perfect. We are not God, and there isn't some imaginary level of Christianity where we become so Holy that we will not make mistakes. Frankly, we are all sinners. Period. While we are all different in one way or another, the one thing we all have in common is the tendency to sin. While we may become more consistent in our relationship with God, we are still far from perfect. It is so important to always remain humble and remember our beginnings. We should never forget that had it not been for the grace and mercy of God, life and situations could be altogether worse. I especially believe it is so important to be transparent with others in an effort to encourage them and remind them that we are all beautifully flawed. Perfection is merely a myth for human beings but a reality only for God.

30- Super Christian

"And now these three remain: faith, hope and love. But the greatest of these is love." (1 Corinthians 13:13)

How do you find that middle ground when you love God, and you are consciously trying to live according to His word, yet you don't want to come across as some know-it-all super-Christian? Well, we should never feel compelled to deny our faith or stance on issues simply because we don't want to make other people uncomfortable. However, we should approach all situations with love and from a place of humility. As Christian stewards, we shouldn't be quick to always correct people or overwhelm them with what the gospel says. Being a friend to someone isn't always about being right or calling people out. If we ever feel led to speak on an issue, we ought to ask God to give us the right opportunity and the right words. Making someone feel bad is not of God. Simply, approach is everything. When we do things in love, there is a greater possibility that people will be open to what we have to say rather than oppositional. Remember, operating in love is a way of reflecting what God's love is all about.

31- Talented Sisters

"We have different gifts, according to the grace given us. If a man's gift is prophesying, let him use it in the proportion to his faith. If it is service, let him serve; if it is teaching, let him teach; if it is encouraging, let him encourage; if it is contributing to the needs of others, let him give generously; if it is leadership, let him govern diligently; if it is showing mercy, let him do it cheerfully." (Romans 12:6-8)

My sister has exceptionally gifted hands. She can draw, she's a hair stylist, she's a photographer, and she is talented on many other fronts. She has so many talents in such a small package! *(She's 3 feet shorter than I am.)* And then, there's me. I found peace in reading and writing as a kid because I was so shy. A good book or a pen and paper kept me pretty satisfied. The problem is, I never looked in the mirror and considered myself a talented person when compared to my sister. Sure, I could write a paper with no issues or finish a 500 page book in no time, but so what? No one was checking for the girl whose head was always stuck in a book or writing her life away.

How many of us dim the light on our own gifts, simply because we don't feel or think we measure up to what others have? Comparison will kill your confidence and keep you from reaching your full potential. It's not worth it. I guarantee that if you take note of the abilities that God has given you and put in the necessary work, it will bring you so much fulfillment. It's not always about being famous or having multiple talents. It is about fully using what God has placed in you. I'll have you know that my sister has blossomed into a successful business owner, and she inspires me whether she realizes it or not. Her gifts are her gifts and my gifts are my gifts. Together, we are talented sisters.

32- Time Management

"Teach us to number our days aright, that we may gain a heart of wisdom." (Psalm 90:12)

The more responsibilities we have, the more it seems like there just aren't enough hours in the day. Somehow, in the midst of everything else we have going on, we also have to make time for God. Now, we might be overwhelmed and stressed out, but giving God the last few sleepy moments of our day is an injustice to ourselves and our relationship with God. We should make an intentional effort to take a look at our schedules and carve out some time to spend with God. Even if you have to turn off the radio in the car to have some quiet time, or do some spiritual reading on your lunch break, it will surely be worth it. Plants that are not watered will eventually die, and relationships that are not nurtured cannot thrive. We have to make each day count so that our relationship with God becomes stronger and more nourished.

33- Don't Be a Hater

"That you may be children of your Father in heaven. He causes His sun to rise on the evil and the good, and sends rain on the righteous and the unrighteous." (Matthew 5:45)

Sometimes it's a bit perplexing to see how people who aren't focused on God are doing very well, but it's not our job to understand. God is in the business of blessing the just and the unjust. The same way people will not always understand what God is doing in our lives, we should never speculate why God is doing something in someone else's life. Yes, maybe you believe that your coworker didn't deserve that promotion, but nothing happens by accident. Maybe that person needs the extra money. Maybe God is going to use that person's previous job to promote someone else who is in a desperate need of a break. It's not our job to question how or why God blesses other people. The bible clearly tells us that God is in the business of blessing all people, whether they realize from whom their blessings come from or not.

34- Room to Breathe

"Do not keep talking so proudly or let your mouth speak such arrogance, for the Lord is a God who knows, and by Him deeds are weighed." (1 Samuel 2:3)

I have learned that not everyone is going to think like I think. Not everyone is going to approach problems like I do. The way we choose to individually do something may not be right for the next person. When we start to tell ourselves that we know what's best for other people and we have all the answers for everyone's problems, that's exactly when we need to take a step back. Sometimes we might want to shake someone into realizing that they aren't making the right decision. However, we all have to go through circumstances not only to learn about ourselves, but to discover more about God. We have to give people room to breathe, room to grow, and room to make mistakes. Moreover, if we feel compelled to give advice, we shouldn't speak recklessly but rather pray and ask God for the right words.

35- Love God's Way

"Love is patient, love is kind. It does not envy, it does not boast, it is not proud. It is not rude, it is not self-seeking, it is not easily angered, it keeps no record of wrongs. Love does not delight in evil but rejoices with the truth. It always protects, always trusts, always hopes, always perseveres." (1 Corinthians 13:4-7)

No relationship or friendship can last through hard times without love. The world's definition of love is a far cry from how the bible commands us to love. As Christians, we are the examples for the rest of the world of what the love of God looks like. To treat others with hate or disgust is so far from the love God expects us to show others. When we fall into the trap of being hateful towards someone for whatever reason (and sometimes it's pure nonsense), we are sinning. We have to be careful of putting stipulations on when to be kind and loving towards others. While we may not always get it right, we have to make a conscious effort to love genuinely, because God is love.

36- The Criteria

"Above all, love each other deeply; because love covers a multitude of sins." (1 Peter 4:8)

Some friends are meant to stay in the past, while other friendships have to end temporarily to flourish in the future. And then, there are friendships that seem so effortless, and they are meant to last a lifetime. I am thankful for all my true friends - the ones I trust without question. I hope you have at least one or two true friends of your own. While we are not perfect people, we must support each other, love each other, and respect each other. Let us be inclined to apologize, be supportive, and compassionate. We should be mindful that the other person has their own responsibilities and probably wears multiple hats. Let us not pretend to have all the answers and love one another unconditionally. This is the criteria for long-lasting friendships.

37- Shine for Jesus

"You are the light of the world. A city on a hill cannot be hidden. Neither do people light a lamp and put it under a bowl. Instead they put it on its stand, and it gives light to everyone in the house. In the same way, let your light shine before men, that they may see your good deeds and praise your Father in heaven." *(Matthew 5:14-16)*

Whether we realize it or not, we have a responsibility to be an example. As Christians, our actions should be set apart from the actions of others. How we react to situations should be different. Sure it might logically make sense to go off on someone who is downright rude or mistreat someone because they rubbed us the wrong way, but this only makes sense to the flesh and not the Holy Spirit. How we speak to people should be different. No, we won't always get it right, but we should intentionally seek to be an example of Christ. Matthew 5:14-16 tells us that when we do good deeds, it is a reflection of God. When we respond in love, it is a reflection of God. When we help others, it is a reflection of God. Be a light in this world, and be an example of Christ.

38- Finding Your Purpose

"For I know the plans I have for you," declares the Lord, "plans to prosper you and not to harm you, plans to give you hope and a future. (Jeremiah 29:11)

Sometimes it might seem like everyone else around us is on a path to doing great things, while we're just going through the motions. We start to ask ourselves if nothing great or significant will ever happen in our lives. We may even doubt if putting in hard work to accomplish something is even worth it. Well, it is worth it. The bible tells us that God does have a future for us. God wants to see His children do well in life. He gets no pleasure from seeing any of His children struggle through life. We can rest on God's promise that we indeed have a future, but we have to be wise in our decisions, patient when we pray for guidance, and determined to see our goals come to pass. If you aren't sure what your purpose is, don't hesitate to ask God. Ask Him to reveal it to you, and He will surely give you an answer.

The drive inside of you is no accident. That tugging at your heart is not by chance. Every dream you have can come true. Believe in your talents. Believe that God can and will make it happen. Have the courage to live on purpose. Yes, you might be starting out with just a dream and an idea, but you already have the most important contact, Jesus Christ. Find confidence in being God's child, and know that He is your biggest cheerleader. Today is the perfect time to intentionally pursue the goals God has put on your heart. Educate yourself. Give your talents to God. Claim in the name of Jesus that it will be done. Don't delay your destiny one more day.

Your talents were given to you by God. It wasn't by accident or chance because your talents have purpose.

39-Judgment Day

"Why do you look at the speck of sawdust in your brother's eye and pay no attention to the plank in your own eye? How can you say to your brother, 'Let me take the speck out of your eye,' when all the time there is a plank in your own eye." (Matthew 7:3-4)

The one trait that we all have in common is sin, there is no denying that. With that being said, it's not our duty to highlight other people's sin yet minimize our own because we think it's "not so bad." We should never look down on someone for making the wrong move, because there will be a time when we do just the same. If we spend so much time focusing on how other people are living, when will we have time to focus on being better Christians ourselves? In Matthew 7:2, the bible tells us that in the same way we judge others, we will also be judged. There will come a day when we will all have to answer for our choices in life, so let's leave the judging until Judgment Day. Instead, we should spend less time critiquing others and more time focusing on our personal walk with God.

40- Troubles Don't Last Always

"Peace I leave with you; my peace I give you. I do not give to you as the world gives. Do not let your hearts be troubled and do not be afraid." (John 14:27)

For the woman in a season of loss, hurt, and/or frustration, I want to remind you that seasons do change. Yes, we have to go through some things to learn to trust in God, but remember that you won't always be where you are. According to scripture, there is a time for everything and a season for every activity under Heaven. The good news is that circumstances may change, but who God is will always be constant. I love that about God! Our whole world could be falling apart right before our eyes, but we can always find peace in God. Don't let one season of strife cause you to lose hope. Find peace in knowing that troubles don't last always.

41- She Laughs

"She is clothed with strength and dignity; she can laugh at the days to come." (Proverbs 31:25)

God desires for us to go through life believing first in Him, but also in ourselves. To be strong is to be confident. To be clothed in dignity is to take pride in oneself. We should tackle life with the attitude that we will do great things in this life. To laugh at the days to come means that we are not living in fear of what could be or might not be. You should speak positive things over your life every single day. Tell yourself daily that you are successful, no matter what your current situation looks like. Call out those things you believe for yourself. Smile, because your future is bright.

42- God's Perfect Timing

"Wait for the Lord; be strong and take heart and wait for the Lord." (Psalm 27:14)

Maybe it's just me, but every time I ever settled in life was because I was fearful of what the outcome would be. I told myself things wouldn't work out in my favor, so instead of letting God's plans reveal itself in due time, I handled it my way. I kissed the guy that I wasn't supposed to kiss. I took the job without consulting God. I put myself in compromising situations, because I told myself that I couldn't wait. I just couldn't be patient. I had to have it when I wanted it - whatever the "it" was at the time. How many of us have this idea of what our life is supposed to be like? We tell ourselves we have to get married by a certain age or have a certain number of kids. What if our plans don't fall in line with God's plans? We put our lives on a schedule, but many times, we don't always get what we pray for when we ask for it. God could also give us a big fat NO, not to hurt us, but to protect us. There is something about knowing that God has a plan. We don't have to settle for the "right now". Rather, we need to practice patience and wait on God. His timing is always the best timing.

43- A Love that Never Dies

"And I am convinced that nothing can separate us from God's love. Neither death nor life, neither angels nor demons, neither our fears for today nor our worries about tomorrow, not even the powers of hell can separate us from God's love. No power in the sky above or in the earth below – indeed, nothing in all creation will ever be able to separate us from the love of God that is revealed in Jesus our Lord." (Romans 8:38-39 NLT)

There is a love that cannot be matched. It exceeds every mistake we have ever made and every sin we have committed. It takes precedence over every stronghold you struggle with and every wrong turn you've made. We can drift so far away from God, and He will still love us. Despite everything we have done and will do that is contrary to His word, His love will remain true. His grace and mercy cannot be matched. This is the type of love worth chasing after. This is the type of love that will wipe our tears away, make our fears disappear, and bring light to dark situations. Always remember that no matter how far you might drift from God, you are still loved. No matter how much you wish you could turn back the hands of time to right some wrongs, God still loves you. His love is given freely and is available to anyone - even you!

44- Self Love

"For you formed my inward parts; you knitted me together in my mother's womb. I praise you, for I am fearfully and wonderfully made. Wonderful are your works; my soul knows it very well. My frame was not hidden from you, when I was being made in secret, intricately woven in the depths of the earth." (Psalm 139:14-15 ESV)

We all have insecurities. Even the most beautiful girl with the perfect body has insecurities. Every celebrity on the cover of a magazine has insecurities. They may not blast it on the internet, but it's there because they're human just like you and I. How can God truly shape how we view ourselves, if our culture is so mesmerized by beauty that is airbrushed? Comparing ourselves to this world's idea of beauty is foolish. While we may all have something we want to change about ourselves, the key is not allowing our insecurities to rule our lives and keep us from being our very best.

The bible tells us that even in our mother's womb, God knew us. He created us. This means you weren't created to live in a bubble. You were created to live feeling proud of who you are and what you look like. There are people who live their entire lives and never learn to be comfortable in their own skin. Coming from someone who has struggled with low self-esteem, it's not a fun place to be. While there is nothing wrong with self-improvement, I encourage you to start loving yourself right now. The fact is, self-love is an inside job. If we don't take the time to learn to love who we are, it can keep us from being who we are meant to be.

45- Dead Relationships

"A time to seek, a time to lose; a time to keep, and a time to cast away." (Ecclesiastes 3:6 ESV)

It makes no sense to pray for a dead situation. That relationship was over a long time ago, but you're still praying and asking God to make everything okay. That friendship died a year ago, but you're still holding on because you're so used to hurting each other. God will give us every sign under the sun that it's time to walk away from a situation, but we will ignore Him because it's not what we want to hear. Sometimes it's almost like we live off of unnecessary drama. We get used to it, and without it, things seem off. We know that person is going to disappoint us. We know that person is never going to respect us. Yet, we keep on chasing after something we know is not good for us. I've done it, and I know many others who have as well. Praying for something to live when it died a long time ago is a complete waste of time. So, let me ask you, what is dead in your life that you are still holding on to? It is time to let go of that dead relationship, situation, bad habit, or whatever it may be. Remember, what is dead should be buried.

46- A Seat at The Table

"Being confident of this very thing, that He which hath begun a good work in you will perform it until the day of Jesus Christ." (Philippians 1:6 KJV)

There are some women who are just born with a spark. When they walk into a room, people instantly gravitate to them like a moth to a light. They are confident, beautiful, and maybe even unstoppable. Whether you relate to this woman or not, I have learned that we all bring something to the table. We may not all look the same, dress the same, or speak the same, but we all have something unique about us that makes us who we are. We can go our entire lives admiring everyone else and never give ourselves credit for the greatness that we have to offer. There is no benefit to beating ourselves up. Sometimes, we need to show ourselves a little grace. Understand that it's okay to mess up sometimes, and one disappointment doesn't make you a failure. Sure, there might be a million and one things going on in your life right now, and you may not know if you're coming or going. You just need to prioritize, turn your greatness up a notch, and take things one day at a time.

47- Best Friends Forever

"A friend loves at all times, and a brother is born for adversity."
(Proverbs 17:17)

At some point in your life, you might wake up and your circle of friends will look very different. You used to talk to them all the time, and there wasn't a day that went by when you didn't at least say a quick hello. You laughed and shared secrets, and you knew without a doubt that you would be best friends for life. Then, life happened and people got busy. Priorities changed and interests evolved. The grind got real, and distance followed. Conversations became few and far between, and neither of you could pinpoint the exact time or date when things started to change. Sound familiar? Well, I've been there, too.

Friendships can be tricky as we get older. People find themselves in different seasons of life. For example, you might be single while your best friend is married or vice versa. We individually take on new responsibilities, and sometimes our careers are in very different places. When one person is seeing success, the other might be struggling through life. I've learned firsthand that for one reason or another, some friendships are meant to last forever, while others have to end in order to grow in the future.

Take a look at the people around you. Are you loving towards one another? Are you forgiving? Are you there for each other when things get rough? While all friendships may not look the same, we certainly cannot get so wrapped up in our own lives that we forget to show the people that we care for how much we love and appreciate them. Yes, life gets busy, but don't forget to be a good friend, especially to the people who have been good to you.

48- Embracing the Season

"For the Lord God is a sun and shield; the Lord bestows favor and honor; no good thing does He withhold from those whose walk is blameless." (Psalm 84:11)

When you're single, everyone wants to know when you're getting in a relationship or married. And, I've been around enough married couples to know that once you get married, there will be people who will ask you when you plan on having kids. Seasons change, and sometimes they change without us really embracing the season we were in previously. While every season of life comes with its own burdens and trials, there is something about enjoying where we are in life and not being pressured to move on to the next chapter. There might be some things going on in your life right now that you don't understand or may not like, but I am sure that if you take a step back, you can appreciate at least one thing in your life.

I don't know about you, but I'm not caught up in imaginary milestones that society tells me I have to meet. I strongly believe that as women of faith, we should enjoy the beauty of where we are rather than stress about the future. The bible reminds us that God will never withhold anything from His children. Don't worry yourself about what might not happen for you when that time hasn't even come. Instead of focusing on what you don't have or listening to people put ideas in your head, focus on seeking God. He sees when you are being intentional. He knows when you are making a sincere effort. That should be your focus.

49- Remain Humble

"Naked I came from my mother's womb, and naked I depart. The Lord gave and the Lord has taken away; may the name of the Lord be praised." (Job 1:21)

As we progress in life, it is so important for us to always remain humble. Yes, you've been putting in those extra hours and that promotion was well-deserved. Yes, you are on your way to completing your degree and you've got a great job lined up. Your small victories have led to big victories, and things are headed in the right direction for you. So the question becomes, how should we respond to success? It's simple: we remain grateful and always remember from whom our blessings originated. In the bible, Job reminds us that we came into this world with nothing. Sure, we may have paid for everything we have, but who blessed us with the ability to do so? God. When God blesses us, our actions should be a display of gratitude. Boasting and having an attitude of entitlement are not a reflection of being grateful. The fact is that what God gives us, He can surely take away.

50- God's Power

"Ah, Sovereign Lord, you have made the heavens and earth by your great power and outstretched arm. Nothing is too hard for you." (Jeremiah 32:17)

There are many characteristics of God, but one that I find extraordinary is His power. Why is that? I'm glad you asked. The God we serve can do anything. He can fix any problem. As we live our lives and face trials, we have to learn to rest in the fact that our God is more powerful than any problem we can ever face. Believing this is just the first step, because we then have to live by it. No more should we let life's problems beat us down. We should live our lives knowing that there is no situation that God can't save us from when we need Him. He is sovereign and powerful, and He is God. We must take the time to just sit down in a quiet place and reflect on who God is, not our problems, wants, or needs, but just who He is – AMAZING.

51- From 0 -10

"My dear brothers, take note of this: Everyone should be quick to listen, slow to speak and slow to become angry, for man's anger does not bring about the righteous life that God desires."
(James 1:19-20)

We all have triggers that take our attitudes or moods from zero to ten in a matter of seconds. Obviously, getting angry and losing control of our emotions is never a good thing. So here is a thought. What if we listened more, spoke less, and controlled our emotions when we face those triggers? Will it be easy? Absolutely not, but nothing God calls us to do is easy. The next time you run into that person who just works your last nerve, and there is no getting around speaking to that person, just try your best to practice self-control. Whether you have to count to ten, say a quick prayer, or so forth, make the effort to control your anger because God will honor that.

52- Right or Wrong

"When pride comes, then comes disgrace, but with humility comes wisdom." (Proverbs 11:2)

I have had many dysfunctional relationships, and as a result, many people have come and gone throughout my life. When I look back on the role I played in some of those relationships, I can admit that I didn't always show the type of love that God calls us to show to others. There were times when I completely went off, and there were times when I cut people off with no warning. In some situations, I told myself that I was right with no ifs, ands, or buts about it. In retrospect, I had to acknowledge the fact that it isn't always about being right or wrong. When we put our pride aside, we just might learn something about ourselves and the person we are at odds with. Conflict is never fun but if we can learn something, then it's not in vein.

53-Forgiveness

"And when you stand praying, if you hold anything against any-one, forgive him, so that your Father in heaven may forgive you your sins." (Mark 11:25)

Has someone ever made you so mad that you made a promise to yourself that you would never speak to them ever again? Did someone very close to you disappoint you, and you've never been the same? Has your heart ever been broken? What did you do with that hurt? If days, weeks, or even years have passed by, and you are still hurting, it's time to forgive. I've definitely had my fair share of heart break and disappointment. There was a time in when my response to someone hurting me was to cut them off with no warning. I now understand that not only was that selfish, but it was also like putting a band aid on the real issue that required stitches to heal.

When we walk around unable to forgive, it can spread like a wildfire. It can totally disrupt our lives, even if we are unable to recognize it. There's the potential to become bitter and angry, while the person you are mad at is not even thinking about you. Friends or even your family may see a change in your attitude and demeanor. You take on this pessimistic view of life and put up a wall, making it hard for anyone to have a smooth conversation with you. Meanwhile, the root of all of this could very well be that someone hurt you and you just can't let it go. Unfortunately, there are no stipulations for forgiveness. You may never get an apology, and your hurt feelings may never be acknowledged, but that's okay. Forgiveness is about you leaving your past where it is; it's not about the other person.

I don't know about you, but I fall sometimes. I don't always make the right decisions, and I need God's forgiveness! Forgiveness doesn't mean that you have to speak to that person every day. It does not mean that because you have let it go, you have to the best of friends. It simply means that you are no longer keeping that situation in your heart. I urge you to work on this, if it is something that you struggle with in your life. Begin to pray today and ask God to cleanse your heart. Decide at this very moment as you are reading that you will no longer be controlled by what someone did to you. When we forgive, it frees us while releasing the person we have forgiven.

54-The Bold and The Courageous

"Have I not commanded you? Be strong and courageous. Do not be terrified; do not be discouraged, for the Lord your God will be with you wherever you go." (Joshua 1:9)

Let me paint a picture for you. You want to go back to school, but you've decided not tell anyone for fear that they will surely ask when you will enroll. Better yet, maybe you've been working on a project for months, and it's finally ready, but you haven't done anything with it because you're afraid of the feedback you might get. To be bold means to take risks. To be bold means setting deadlines and making sure you meet them. Being bold means marketing yourself and not being afraid to tell people who you are and what you do. Be bold and courageous! It's one thing to talk about it, but it's another thing to do it expecting great results!

55- God's Property

"Do you not know that your bodies are temples of the Holy Spirit, who is in you, whom you have received from God? You are not your own." (1 Corinthians 6:19)

Living a healthy lifestyle can be a hard thing, especially when you absolutely love sweets like I do. We are reminded by this scripture that our bodies are not our own, and when we put unhealthy things into it, we are not taking very good care of God's property. This isn't about sneaking in a piece of cake from time to time, or even about being at a certain fitness level. We all should take care of our bodies, and individually focus on how we can be healthier in our day to day lives. May I add that through Christ we can do anything, and that includes making healthier choices? It might take some pure determination to walk away from that piece of cake or our favorite dish, but it can be done. Pray for strength and discipline each day to make better decisions. And, if you are on a fitness journey or thinking about it, take God along you!

56- Unstoppable

"What, then, shall we say in response to these things? If God is for us, who can be against us?" (Romans 8:31)

Confidence starts within your heart and mind. It does not begin with our outward appearance or worldly possessions. When life throws us a curve ball, we have to remain confident because we know God is with us. Confidence is when you dress for the job you want, speak that promotion into existence, or envision that degree up on the wall. Whatever you want to accomplish in life, know that there isn't a devil in hell that can stop you unless you let them. Walk with your head held high, because you know you deserve the best and can achieve your goals in life. How we maneuver through life is largely based on how we perceive ourselves. So, from this day forward, I want you to believe in yourself even if the people around you don't! I want you to believe in yourself even if you don't know the how or the when. There might be roadblocks, but you are a conqueror. You have the ability to be unstoppable because God lives in you!

57- Broaden Your Horizons

"This is what God the Lord says —He who created the heavens and stretched them out, who spread out the earth and all that comes out of it, who gives breath to its people, and life to those who walk it." (Isaiah 42:5)

There is nothing like taking a flight during the day and literally seeing the world from a different vantage point. It is a true reminder of just how big and how beautiful this world is. There is so much to see and so much to explore. Just imagine that every place you ever visit was created by God. The beauty and the culture of every city, state, country, and continent will broaden your scope on life. Get out and see the world. Don't limit yourself to your neighborhood or people who look just like you. We limit our perspective when we don't expose ourselves to different cultures and ways of life. If your funds are limited, set short term financial goals so you can one day take the trip of your dreams. I'm blessed that my family is from Trinidad. When I visited for the first time, I was in awe of the beauty of the country. It was a true reminder that this world stretches far past the neighborhood that we come from or live in right now. Live. Explore. Don't limit your perspective.

58-What's My Purpose?

"For I know the plans I have for you," declares the LORD, "plans to prosper you and not to harm you, plans to give you hope and a future." (Jeremiah 29:11)

I have a friend named Jennifer who took a cookie decorating class a few years ago, only to realize she had a natural talent for decorating cookies. One class sparked her interest, and now through her cookies, she is able to put a smile on so many people's faces. When she walked into that bakery to take her class, she didn't know that she was literally walking into her destiny. Isn't it funny how God will reveal things to us when we least expect it? Her story is a true testament that God has a purpose for all of us. We have a destiny that has already been planned. The seed has been planted. The potential is there whether you are able to recognize it or not. If you are wondering what your purpose is in life, trust that when the time is right, God will reveal it.

59- Weather the Storm

"Then He got into the boat and His disciples followed him. Without warning, a furious storm came up on the lake, so that the waves swept over the boat. But Jesus was sleeping. The disciples went and woke Him, saying, "Lord, save us! We're going to drown!" He replied, "You of little faith, why are you so afraid?" Then He got up and rebuked the winds and the waves, and it was completely calm. The men were amazed and asked, "What kind of man is this? Even the winds and the waves obey him!" (Matthew 8:23-27)

Fighting the same battles over and over again is not fun. You keep having the same arguments with the same person. If you're single, you seem to keep dating the same kind of guys that bring no value to your life. Money is looking funny, and you're tired of calling upon other people to help you pay your bills. The vicious cycles we find ourselves in are hardly an accident. God just might be testing you to see if you are ready to handle what He has planned for you.

There is a lesson to be learned from where you are today, that is preparing you for tomorrow. In every situation we face, we can learn something about God, as well as ourselves. The lessons we learn during the storms are what keep us strong when the storm passes, and prepares us for the plans God has already made. Don't miss the opportunity to learn a lesson disguised in a storm. Embrace the opportunity, learn the lesson, and get ready for the next one. Remember, sometimes we receive God's best by way of suffering and pain, followed by a strong dose of love or perhaps the next storm.

60- People Pleasers and God Pleasers

"His master replied, "Well done, good and faithful servant! You have been faithful with a few things; I will put you in charge of many things. Come and share your master's happiness!"
(Mathew 25:23)

Helping people is one thing, but always trying to please people is another. Depending on who the person is, we might hesitate to say no. In other cases, we take on way more than we can handle, simply because we either don't want to disappoint someone or we don't want to go through the hassle of having to provide further explanation. Well, as much as we strive to please people, we should really strive to please God as well. When we make serving God a priority, we make the conscious effort to please Him first and foremost. How about we try to put a smile on God's face by being obedient? What would happen if we diligently worked towards pleasing Him in our actions, our attitude, and our thoughts? I'd like to think that we would make God happy. When that sky cracks open, and I behold the presence of God, I want Him to look down on me and say, "Well done, good and faithful servant!" How about you?

61- So Close, Yet So Far Away

"I have fought the good fight, I have finished the race, I have kept the faith. Now there is in store for me the crown of righteousness, which the Lord, the righteous Judge, will award me on that day – and not only to me, but to all who have longed for his appearing." (2 Timothy 4:7-8)

There is nothing like almost crossing the finish line only to fall on your face at crunch time. Disappointments will either push us to finish what we started, or cause us to walk away defeated. You may feel embarrassed by those disappointments, but remember that while you may have run into a stumbling block, you are closer to your dream than you were maybe a month or even a year ago. Feeling disappointed is normal, but don't stay there, because that would just be way too easy. No matter how difficult things may get, the bible tells us that we can do anything through Christ. So assess the situation, dust yourself off, ask yourself what you can learn, and get back to it. If you have to pray for strength every minute on the minute, then do so, but don't give up!

62- Giving and Worship

"Bring the full tithe into the storehouse, that there may be food in my house. Test me in this," says the Lord Almighty, "and see if I will not throw open the floodgates of heaven and pour out so much blessing that you will not have room enough for it." (Malachi 3:10)

If you've ever attended a church, you've witnessed the time in the service when the offering bucket goes around. And, maybe you wondered if you should give or not. Although I grew up in church, I didn't understand the value of giving offering and tithes until I was out on my own and building a stronger relationship with God. Rather than look at offering and tithes as a burden, I realized that it is indeed a form of worship. The topic of tithing and giving offering can be sliced and diced in many different ways, and I wouldn't dare tackle the ins and outs in a short devotional. What I do want to do, is to encourage you to get to a place where you understand the purpose.

For me, tithing is a way of giving back to God a small portion of what He gave us. Like all things, it requires faith. Do you believe that God can and will open up the floodgates of Heaven and bless you far beyond every prayer you have ever prayed? Do you believe that He has the power to blow your mind in every aspect of your life? You know your situation. If you don't routinely give or tithe in church, I encourage you to study the purpose behind it. Study the origin and importance of it. Consider the fact that while we ought to give because of all God has done for us, when we are faithful to God He will honor that.

63- I am Free

"But because of His great love for us, God, who is rich in mercy, made us alive with Christ even when we were dead in transgressions – it is by grace you have been saved."(Ephesians 2:4-5)

Oh, where would we be without the grace of God?! When Jesus Christ died on the cross, He paid the ultimate price for our sins. It was on that day that we became free and blameless. You don't have to walk around with a heavy heart because you don't always get it right. God's grace is sufficient. Each morning God gives us grace to see another day. It's because of grace that we have survived the situations that we have experienced. Just think, each and every day, God shows us grace by blessing us and protecting us when we struggle with sin. No, we don't deserve it, but He shows us grace anyway. In trying to model our lives according to God's word, let us be thankful for the grace God shows us and be mindful to show grace to others daily.

64- The Power of Words

"Let no corrupting talk come out of your mouths, but only such as is good for building up, as fits the occasion, that it may give grace to those who hear." (Ephesians 4:29 ESV)

Words do hurt. There is no philosophical explanation needed. When it comes to day to day interactions, words have the power to lift someone's spirits or completely ruin their day. Words have the power to encourage or to discourage. Words have the power to give hope or encourage defeat. In a perfect world, everyone is going to be kind, and we're all going to respond to one another in the right way; however, perfection doesn't exist. Furthermore, there are even people in adulthood who are still scarred by words that were spoken to them as children.

I can remember being teased as early as elementary school, and as I went through grade school, I was convinced that I just wasn't pretty enough. I let people's mean comments make me feel like I didn't matter. From dysfunctional relationships as I grew older to shying away from opportunities, it took me a long time to get to a new place within myself. In essence, words spoken to me as a child almost kept me from being who I wanted to be as a woman and who God intended for me to be as a child. Even as grown women, we should be mindful of what comes out of our mouths. We should think before we speak and be conscious of how we make others feel, because our words have power.

65- Kindness is Not a Weakness

"Be kind and compassionate to one another, forgiving each other, just as in Christ God forgave you." (Ephesians 4:32)

In this day and age, gentleness is seen as a sign of weakness while yelling is seen as a sign of strength. Well, I beg to differ. It takes spiritual strength to respond in love when someone is being rude, or to show mercy to someone who has used us. It takes spiritual strength to forgive someone for hurting us in the worst way. It takes spiritual strength to keep pushing when we have every reason to give up. Kindness is not a weakness. Instead, kindness is an act of strength and humility that is pleasing to God. In fact, it is so much easier to act in anger than it is to muscle up the strength to remain kind in a world that constantly temps you to be revengeful and unforgiving. Practice being kind and forgiving just as God has done for us.

66- Money Hungry

"Whoever can be trusted with very little can also be trusted with much, and whoever is dishonest with very little will also be dishonest with much." (Luke 16:10)

Wanting more when we cannot handle what we already have is never a good thing. You might be praying for something right now, but you aren't managing the things you already have. Whether it is money, authority, or how you choose to get ahead in life, we should be honest and mindful of how we manage the things that God has given us.

Specifically when it comes to money, I want to add that there are so many people in debt because they want to impress others. Meanwhile, the person they're trying to impress is living in debt as well. We have to learn to be content with what we have and live within our means. If we don't have the money to spend, we don't need to buy it. Don't put yourself in a position to struggle or to live paycheck to paycheck. Ask God for discipline in this area, but couple that with making better financial decisions. Moreover, don't be too prideful to seek the necessary help to get your financial situation on track. Most people on this earth have made at least one bad financial decision. Get the help you need if you need it. When you do right by the things God has given to you, watch how much more abundantly you will be blessed.

67- Filling Voids

"May the God of hope fill you will all the joy and peace as you trust in him, so that you may overflow with hope by the power of the Holy Spirit." (Romans 15:13)

Sometimes we feel as though our lives are missing something, and we run to the first thing that will make us feel better. However, people and things will never fill voids for very long. We all have that thing or possibly a person who can provide us with that temporary comfort. The truth is that God should fill those voids in our lives. When we are feeling like we are not enough or that our lives are lacking something, we should go to God for clarity and understanding. God is whoever and whatever we need Him to be. His presence can fill any void in our lives.

Is there a void in your life? What are you doing to fill this void? Who or what is the void filler that you need to replace with God? This might require you to sit down and really evaluate some things in your life. It may not be easy, especially when we keep running to the same thing. It's not just about being delivered from something, but understanding why we do the things we do so that we can live better lives.

68- Who, What, When, and Where

"A perverse man stirs up dissension and a gossip separates close friends." (Proverbs 16:28)

As ladies, we can admit that dinner, wine, and some good old gossip has taken place at some point in our lives. However, it's all fun and games until the tables turn and people sit around and start gossiping about us! This happened to me, and it changed my perspective on discussing other people's business. I think to some degree, people can have a natural curiosity, and sometimes it's out of concern and not being nosey. Either way, as we mature, so should our conversations. We should be talking about our goals, dreams, and aspirations. We should be so busy working on ourselves, our relationship with God, and trying to better ourselves, that we don't have time to figure out the who, what, when, and where of someone else's life. At the end of the day, nothing good comes from gossiping. It only creates division, confusion, and conflict.

69- No New Friends

"A friend loves at all times, and a brother is born for adversity."
(Proverbs 17:17)

I don't care how independent and strong you are as a woman, we all need somebody. I used to be of the belief that with the exception of my parents, I didn't need friends. I'd had enough failed friendships that I didn't desire to be close to anyone. What I didn't know was that eventually life would happen, and who wants to go through hell and not have someone to depend on? I've heard many women say, "Girl, I just keep to myself because people can't be trusted." Yes, people will disappoint us, but we also have the potential to disappoint others.

Friendship is important, and we weren't created to live in isolation. We were created to live in community with each other. There is this misconception that as we get older, we don't need any new friends. Well, sometimes God will put people in our lives that treat us far better than people we have known our entire lives. Making new friends might push you to get out of your comfort zone, but it's well worth it. In seeking genuine friendship, let us be aware that we ourselves may need to be that genuine friend to someone else.

70- Pray Without Ceasing

"Be joyful always; pray continually; give thanks in all circum-stances, for this is God's will for you in Christ Jesus."
(1 Thessalonians 5:16)

What are you to do when you are praying, yet your situation isn't getting any better? Or, you're spending significant time with God, but it just seems like you can't catch a break? The bible tells us that we are commanded to remain joyful during tough times, to give thanks no matter what we are going through, and most importantly, to keep on praying. Developing a strong prayer life means praying even when we may not feel like it or when it seems like it's not working. It means giving our situation to God instead of tossing and turning at night because we're trying to fig-ure it out ourselves. Praying isn't about using fancy words or say-ing the perfect prayer. Remember that God already knows what's going on in your life. He just wants you to reach out to Him and to depend on Him. So, don't stop praying. Don't throw in the towel. If you have to pray every hour on the hour, then a girl has to do what she has to do!

71- Flesh Eater

"For our struggle is not against flesh and blood, but against the rulers, against the authorities, against the powers of this dark world and against the spiritual forces of evil in the heavenly realms." (Ephesians 6:12)

The flesh wants what it wants, and the only way to control our fleshly desires is through the Spirit. If our actions and our words are not led by the Spirit, that means they are led by the flesh. How do we learn to tame our flesh when the devil is constantly raising hell in our lives? We do so when we study and apply God's word. Remember, the devil doesn't sleep. He is on a mission to distract us and take us off our course. He knows all too well that the flesh is hungry for whatever it desires.

There is a constant battle between our flesh and the Spirit. Particularly when we deal with people issues, we have to remember that the issue may not be with the person. It could be that the person isn't being led by the Spirit, yet our flesh leads us to believe otherwise. The best thing we can do in situations like this is to pray for that person and focus on our own spirit. Now, I'll admit that this is sometimes a difficult choice, but the more we focus on feeding the Spirit and not our flesh, the more equipped we are to be led by the Spirit to do only that which the Spirit is able to do.

72 - Delight Yourself in the Lord

"Delight yourself in the Lord and He will give you the desires of your heart." (Psalm 37:4)

There was a time when I interpreted this scripture as if God was a snack machine. I thought it meant, if I gave God a little bit of my time, I'd get a little something in return. I have since learned that the quality of my relationship with God is dependent on me knowing who He is. The significance of knowing Him this way, *I mean really knowing Him*, has more to do with understanding what is required of us, rather than what we can get from Him. Knowing Him requires spending quality time with Him. Knowing Him causes our desires to line up with His desires for us. When we delight ourselves in the Lord, we feel true anticipation of studying God's word. It is no longer a chore for us or something that we check off our to-do list, before we are off to tackle the next item on the list.

Do you find great pleasure in spending time with God? Do you enjoy worshiping in His presence simply because of who He is? If you're not there yet, it's okay. We know that prayer and a relationship with God requires discipline. Take things day by day and learn to find peace in God's presence. Remember, when we seek God with a sincere heart, it cultivates a trust and assurance that God will give us the desires of our hearts.

73- A Gift that Keeps on Giving

"For everything that was written in the past was written to teach us, so that through endurance and the encouragement of the Scriptures we might have hope." (Romans 15:4)

The word of God will always remain true. It is not a storybook full of fairy tales that has lost its value with time. In fact, it is timeless and relevant. Some would say there is no way a man could walk on water or turn water into wine, but it did indeed happen. While some things will lose its significance as time goes by, the bible will forever be our greatest strength, and we need it now more than ever. Frankly, the world seems to have gone completely crazy, or maybe it's always been crazy and I just didn't realize to what extent. Either way, the bible is our strength in a crazy world, and that means we have to read it to know it in order to live it. It is a source of hope and a gift that keeps on giving.

74- Spirit Led Decisions

"If any of you lacks wisdom, he should ask God, who gives gener-
ously to all without finding fault, and it will be given to him. But
when he asks, he must believe and not doubt, because he who
doubts is like a wave of the sea, blown and tossed by the wind.
That man should not think he will receive anything from the Lord;
he is a double-minded man, unstable in all he does." (James 1:5-8)

Decisions are a part of growing up and the older we get, the
more complicated our decisions become. We can't escape them no
matter how badly we want to take a break from them, especially
the really hard ones. Have you ever had to make a decision and
found yourself going back and forth about it every other day? Better yet, have you made a decision on a whim only to realize you
didn't give it enough thought and it was too late to recant? The
good news is that we can lean on the Holy Spirit to help us make
all kinds of decisions, whether significant or insignificant.

The bible tells us that God is not the author of confusion.
When we are confused, we especially need to seek God before we
make our next move. Emotions will have us all over the place, and
we've established that praying and waiting is no easy task. On the
bright side, when we wait on God and allow Him to speak to our
hearts and minds, we receive clarity. In addition, when we know
better, we can do better later. If you don't make the right decision
today, make a better one tomorrow.

75- The Next Chapter: Going Higher

"But those who hope in the Lord will renew their strength. They will soar on wings like eagles; they will run and not grow weary, they will walk and not be faint." (Isaiah 40:31)

What does the next chapter of your relationship with God look like? Will you seek Him daily? Will you include Him in your daily decisions no matter how small? Will you look in the mirror and see greatness no matter how ugly your past may be? Will you find contentment in the season you are in all while putting in the necessary work to do great things in your next season? My prayer for you and I is that we would go higher every single day. When God is tugging at our hearts, I pray that we will pay attention. It is my hope that we will put Him first and not last. The journey won't be the same for all of us, but we can all go higher together, by encouraging and supporting each other. There is so much inside of us as children of God, and when we are patient, disciplined, and faithful, I have no doubt that our next chapter will be better than our previous.

21 Affirmations

1. I am not my past. Where I've been is not where I'm going. I will not be held captive by past mistakes. Each day I am doing better than I did the day before.
2. My future is bright. God has a purpose for me. There might be trials along the way, but I will get there.
3. I will be an example to others, because God has charged me with being a light in this world.
4. I will never shy away from telling others how good God has been to me.
5. I am the daughter of the Most High. My Father in Heaven lives within me. He will never leave me nor forsake me.
6. I will own my mistakes and make a conscious effort to live better and do better.
7. I will be confident in my strengths, talents, and abilities. Each have been given to me from God, and He has en trusted me with them. I will develop, nurture, and use my talents.
8. I will live a life of expectancy. What God has for me is for me, and there is nothing anyone can do about it.
9. My beauty is not defined by worldly standards. I am beautiful because I was created by God.
10. I will forgive others.
11. I am free in Jesus Christ. He died for my sins and paid the ultimate price for my salvation.
12. I will rest in God's presence. He is all that I need.
13. My joy comes from God and God alone. When things are not going my way, I will trust Him to see me through.
14. I will help others and not tear them down. I will encourage

others and be kind.

15. I will exercise patience in my life daily.
16. I will discipline myself and study the word. In this, I will learn to hear the voice of God.
17. My prayers never fall on deaf ears. In seasons of waiting, I will trust that God hears my prayers and is working on my be half.
18. God's love cannot be matched. Though I fall, God's love remains.
19. I will manage the things God has blessed me with. I am only a steward.
20. I will be bold in pursuing my dreams. I will exercise faith and not focus on what I can see, but on what I can't see.
21. I will intentionally seek God daily and make my relation ship with Him a priority.

You Are

True confidence starts with the mind. Your momma, your daddy, your best friend, your husband, or whomever can tell you all day long that you are enough, but until YOU believe it, those words will just go into one ear and out the other. We will believe what others say about us, but hesitate to focus on how God defines us as His children. How does God see you? I'm glad you asked...

You are a child of God. (John 1:12)

You have been given the Spirit of power, love, and self-discipline. (2 Timothy 1:7)

You have peace with God. (Romans 5:11)

The Holy Spirit lives in you. (1 Corinthians 3:16)

You are justified. (Romans 5:1)

You are Christ's ambassador. (2 Corinthians 5:20)

You have redemption through Christ. (Colossians 1:14)

God loves you. (Jeremiah 31:3)

You are blameless and beyond reproach. (Colossians 1:22)

You are God's friend. (John 15:15)

102

You are chosen by God to bear fruit. (John 15:16)

You are a member of Christ's body. (1 Corinthians 12:27)

You are chosen by God, Holy, and dearly loved. (Colossians 3:12)

You are the salt of the earth. (Matthew 5:13)

You are the light of the world. (Matthew 5:14)

You are hidden with Christ in God. (Colossians 3:3)

You are sanctified. (Hebrews 2:11)

You are a member of a chosen race, a royal priesthood, a holy nation, a people for God's own possession, and created to sing His praises. (1 Peter 2:9-10)

You are born of God, and the evil one cannot touch you. (1 John 5:18)

You were made complete in Jesus Christ. (Colossians 2:10)

You are God's workmanship. (Ephesians 2:10)

You can do all things through Christ. (Philippians 4:13)

You were beautifully and wonderfully made. (Psalms 139:14)